best new poets
2007

Natasha Trethewey, Editor

Jeb Livingood, Series Editor

This book was published by Samovar Press, Charlottesville, Virginia,
in cooperation with *Meridian,* www.readmeridian.org. For additional information
on *Best New Poets,* see our Web site at www.bestnewpoets.org.

Cover photograph from Crestock.com

Text set in Adobe Garamond Pro

Printed by Thomson-Shore, Dexter, Michigan

ISBN 13: 978-0-9766296-2-7
ISBN 10: 0-9766296-2-3
ISSN 1554-7019

To my brother, Joe, with love
—N.T.

To Jill
—J.L.

Contents

Introduction

Welcome to *Best New Poets 2007*, our third installment of fifty poems from emerging writers. In these pages, the term "emerging writer" has a narrow definition: here, it means someone who has yet to publish a book-length collection of poetry. Like the rules for many anthologies, that one is, perhaps, arbitrary. But the main goal of *Best New Poets* is to provide special encouragement and recognition to new poets, the many writing programs they attend, and the magazines that publish their work. And, of course, to deliver an accessible, eclectic sampling of emerging poets to you, the reader.

From April to June of 2007, *Best New Poets* accepted nominations from each of the above sources. For a small reading fee, writers could upload two poems to a Web site, www.bestnewpoets.org, as part of our Open Competition. A month earlier, writing programs from around the United States and Canada had sent nominations of up to two writers, whom *Best New Poets* later solicited for work. And the anthology also asked literary magazines across North America to send two of their best recent poems by writers who met our definition of "emerging." We asked that the poems submitted either be unpublished or published after April 15, 2006. So, not only do new writers appear in this anthology, you're also seeing some of their latest work.

In all, we received almost 1,300 submissions, most of them containing two poems each, for a total of nearly 2,500 poems. Five dedicated readers blindly ranked these submissions, sending 194 poems to this year's editor, Natasha Trethewey, who selected the final fifty. Three Open Competition poets, Liz Gallagher, Ed Madden, and Laura Newbern, also received cash prizes for their outstanding work.

There are many people I should thank, but the most important are the five readers I briefly mentioned above: Joe Chapman, Lilah Hegnauer, Julia Hansen,

Terence Huber, and Sarah Graham. All of them are practicing poets, and I found them to be a very inclusive and diligent bunch—and unafraid to disagree and fight for a poem they liked.

But as with any selection process that takes thousands of entries and distills them down to a very small number of "winners," there is a huge percentage of poems that did not make it into this book. The temptation, then, is to search in these pages for some sort of pattern in theme or style, or to count up how many pages our winning poems run and calculate the average length we favor. Yet such efforts are bound to be fruitless because their implicit assumption is that this anthology (or any other) applies some formula for selection, some quantitative mode of evaluation. Such ideas are, in my opinion, first cousins to the claim that today's writing programs and literary magazines force modern poetry along a very narrow, prescriptive path.

I find such thinking odd at a time when technology and the Internet enables almost any poet to reach a worldwide audience and permits books like this one to be produced on the most modest of budgets. While many major magazines have stopped featuring poetry and turned to true crime or other nonfiction, there are more literary journals in existence today than ever before, each one vying for its own definition of poetry, its own editorial style and aesthetic. And each day, the Internet fosters small communities of like-minded poets and allows them to gather online. If a writing program doesn't appreciate a style of poetry, surely there is an Internet blog that does—or it can be created.

These changes in technology also make it difficult for an anthology like this one to define who it will include, and who it won't. Since 2005, our basic rule has been that only poets who do not yet have a first book in print are eligible to submit to *Best New Poets*. Yet with print-on-demand sites like Lulu.com or amazon.com's createspace, the next question becomes, do you mean published by a publisher, or do you also mean self-published? Does it matter if the book was sold commercially or not? What about an e-book? If my poem was published once in print, and then on the Internet, which publication date matters? Defining eligibility rules in such an environment is like building a house on sand.

We run into a similar problem when we refer to poets as "emerging." Our cover photos have always implied a young group of writers appears in these pages, and for the most part, this is true. Skim through our contributors' notes and you'll see that many of the poets in this book are still completing graduate degrees. But then you read that C. Wade Bentley has four children and a new grandchild, and you realize that "emerging" and "young" are not actually synonymous. In addition, one of this year's selections came from a poet who died in a tragic car accident two years ago. *Black Warrior Review* was kind enough to nominate Greta Wrolstad's work, which they featured in 2006, and we feel lucky to have it.

So, in the end, trying to quantify what a good poem *is* or *isn't* is surely pointless. Set up a standard, and reality simply moves past it. T.S. Eliot said, "Genuine poetry can communicate before it is understood," and perhaps if there is anything common to our selections, that is it. These are fifty poems that in this small anthology, in this particular year of poetry, stopped us as readers, and made us want to come back again.

—Jeb Livingood
University of Virginia

Liz Gallagher

A Poem That Thinks It Has Joined a Circus

A handkerchief is not an emotional holdall.
A cup of tea does not eradicate all-smothering sensations.
A hands-on approach is not the same as a hand-on-a-shoulder
willing a chin to lift and an upper lip to stiffen.
A forehead resting on fingers does not imply that the grains
of sand in an hourglass have filtered through.
A set of eyes staring into space is not an indictment that the sun
came crashing down in the middle of the night.
A sigh that causes trembling and wobbly knees should be
henceforth and without warning trapped in a bell jar and retrained
to come out tinkling ivories with every gasp.
A poem trying to turn a sad feeling on its head does not constitute
a real poem, it is a can-can poem dancing on a pinhead
and walking a tightrope with arms pressed tightly by its sides.

—Open Competition Prize Winner

Robin Beth Schaer

The Liger

Already it never happened—not the fire,
not the lion. Even the tiger fled,

leaving behind the cub too strange
to be her own, the milk teeth still loose

in his jaw. With chuff and muddled stripes,
a modest mane, he is two cats at once,

a fallow giant, both spans combined.
Not the halfling mule bred for work

or peaches grafted to plums, but a spark formed
in a great loneliness. And soon, he will be gone;

impossible lives are always short, too brief
to name. Only the farmers will remember him,

the apparition that stalked their fields. They offered
mangoes and buffalo, kept the orphan as myth.

—Nominated by The Greensboro Review

Christine Rhein

One of those questions

just made for parties, I suppose, our host, Dave, breaking up
the corners of laughter, corralling us in front of the fireplace.

*If you could choose, would you rather have the power
of invisibility or flight?* The sudden ticking clock meant we

good guests were mulling over options, striving to be right
or clever, except for Sara and Melanie who weren't afraid

to shout *Flight!* and *Me too!*, eager to get back to food, wine, a little
flirting, unlike their husbands, Bruce and Pete, preferring the fantasy

of the question to the fantasy of the party (everyone dressed up
and aglow), delving into *invisibility,* the chance to spy

on their *boss meeting with his boss* or on *stock market insiders,*
to linger *in the middle of a women's locker room,* ideas exposing

the practical among us—*Would our clothes be invisible too?*
Could we carry food, a cell phone? Not get run over?

And can the whole invisibility thing be turned off and on at will?
Dave, resolved into a mute observer, sat grinning, shrugging

even when Roger persisted—*No informed decision*
can be made without knowing if we would be invisible to radar

and heat signatures. Also, if light passes right through you,
it wouldn't hit your retinas, thus rendering you blind. Clearly,

flying is the logical choice. Bruce wasn't about to give up
on that locker room—*How fast and how far can one fly?*

What about bird strikes? Or being sucked into jet engines?
Besides, if I were invisible, I could board any plane I wanted to.

Sara rolled her eyes—*The point of flying, my dear, isn't to get*
somewhere, but to soar, to be free, to see the world anew—

and Marcie sighed, *Being short is almost like being invisible.*
So is getting old, said Tom, *even when you're six feet tall.*

Sad, how locker rooms and diamond heists didn't occur to me,
how I only thought about tickling or kicking a politician

while he's on TV, about cleaning my gutters by floating. Guess
I'd like both powers. Roger started in with his tsk-tsking noises—

Well, if we're going to break the rules, and dream, then I want
useful powers—ESP, the strength of Hercules, teleportation.

Rather than telling him where he could teleport to,
I said, *I've never had one of those dreams where I fly.*

The whole room *oh'd*, pity instantly signing me up:
Flying. Imagine, not ever having to worry about falling

or rush hour, and maybe flight could somehow burn calories too.
Dave jumped up, swung his empty glass, his slurring words—

You're all missing the point, and I can't believe anyone
who claims to pick flying because deep down everyone longs

to be invisible, to figure out what people are really like,
like when they're alone, like my ex for instance, except she's not

alone anymore, and—And Tom put his arm around Dave's shoulder,
said, *I know exactly what you mean. Don't you think it might be best*

to have neither power, both with so many damn responsibilities,
and don't we already have enough of those? Dave nodded,

as we did, grateful to carry our plates to the kitchen,
to the immutable apple pie and coffee we knew how

to savor—like Dave's bear hugs, later at the door, where he stood
a bit teary-eyed, guiding our arms into heavy, wingless coats.

—*Nominated by* Michigan Quarterly Review

Cecily Parks

The Fern Seed

> fern seed: the seed of the fern; once popularly supposed to be
> an invisible seed and to confer invisibility upon its possessor.
> —*Oxford Universal Dictionary*

By the slight dimpling of my palm
I knew I owned it, meat and hull. What meat
I cannot say, except that one swallowing

unfastened me from the eye's sight.
Splendid undress: I lost my elbows first.
What I bodied through bodied through me—

stem or stone, bird or rain—landscapes fathomed
my passage; the offing heeded my oncoming.
At an amble, I entered the house you built

for me. Tongue and groove, threshold and stair:
dishevelment was elsewhere. I found no drawer
unshut, no hair in a fruit cup, and within

the cellar's wettest room, you did your sorting
unceasingly, soothing your fingers with
dove-bodied things. Carpenter, I heard

your hands. And knew that all was as I'd left
it, which was not what I'd expected
in my absence. Nor each dormer level

in each wall, nor the same sag in the hardwood floor
giving beneath my ill-defined feet. In short,
I wanted the house to miss me more, and so

I left, choosing the entrance for my exit.
Goodbye, doorframe; goodbye, sill.
You should be saddened by my gallop

on the uphill, my skirts still riding the clotheshorse.
Love, I was ever your cocksure domestic.
But for my part, I preferred the solitary dwelling.

—*Nominated by* River Styx

Robin Ekiss

Vanitas Mundi

To make perfume from an iris,
    you have to mash the roots
but leave the petals intact,

as in *vanitas mundi,* skeletons
    are made of fruit and flowers,
not the dour bones.

It's this way with any form
    of pleading: *please* begins
with *plea*—linguistic insurgency

driven by a sense of urgency,
    not the sort of error in logic
a "war on terror" implies.

Hidden inside: the ornamental
    edge of understanding,
returned to us through language—

moving, but rootless,
    like spent blood
circling the veins.

The consolation of physics
    is art: scoliotic curve
of the earth, cello

that was Adam's
    first knowledge
of women's pinched waists,

gland of a mussel that dyes
    the emperor's robes
imperial purple. Like hell

or hello, homonym
    or homophone, who prey
on each other's predicate,

what can we know
    of the world
but every measure of regret

carried in a word
    with the gravity of air:
begot, beget, begin.

—*Nominated by* The Virginia Quarterly Review

Laura Newbern

In the Jewish Cemetery

Childhood is like the hibiscus
next to the garbage can, wide opening cone

you miss though it's there, white ear
with lavender hole, so close

to your cheek. My mother leaned over and told me
it was too sacred

to bomb. So I took in,
took with me the old stones, their

marks, the walls that closed in, the fact
that what was left over over the graves

was the piece of the sky they lay
quietly under, periwinkle in color. My mother

was very beautiful, always in navy;
Givenchy, Dior, smelling of ribbed

sweaters and flowers and sometimes telling a thing
so deeply into my ear it would begin

to bloom there. And when we were there
it was twilight, as it is now, and I am

alone in the yard. Or
almost alone, in the yard.

—Open Competition Prize Winner

Matthew Nienow

Six Ways of Looking at the Moon

1.
To the Greeks
moon first meant
month, a way
to measure the shape of time.

The Japanese saw a rabbit
making rice cakes.

2.
It is not the earth
rolling away from light
that matters, it is
what follows—
the sky splayed wide, spread open
with color, blood-
orange nectar,
wet-lipped horizon,
scarlet rising
through the sky's alchemy,

gold learning what it takes to be blue,
and the crescent moon—
hung like a boat made of light,
and sinking.

3.
Thousands of scallops washed
up on the beach,
snapping open and shut,
thirsty mouths
calling after each wave—
a thousand moons
winking in sunlight.

4.
The moon pulls
at water, like curtains drawn
wide, then reaches
inside my wife
and releases
another small moon
and the tide.

5.
Tonight, the sky is spilling
light, becoming the folds
of her skirt, copen blue rising,

the moon,
a curving sliver, sharp
and pale and white as her eye,
that milky arc consuming
the unlit portion of itself,
swallowing me whole.

6.
In a dream, I had a daughter
I called Patience. She held
a cube of sugar on her tongue
just long enough to round
its corners, then smiling,
the small moon rose
like a story
between her lips.

—Open Competition Winner

Brandon Som

Alba: The Archer Yi

Because we are helpless in the affairs
of heaven, we place feathers on arrows.
By dowel, the nock's groove against
its bowstring, the arrow by bird's wing
by archer's sight, by aim, superimposing
what is in hand over what is distant,
we arrive at certain conclusions, the end
of this tale for example: after blight
and the consequent famine, nine of ten
suns fell as dark crows. Of the ways
it is told, there's the account of the emperor,
as the ninth sun lay writhing—dark blood
on dark feathers—placing his hand on
the archer's shoulder, so the slung bow
was lowered, a discretion, the story would
have us believe, that is, finally, this sun,
this light, still with its obsession to travel
while we go on living in its obstruction,
even now, this morning, your shoulder white
as scrimshaw, drawing the light to its fletching.

—Open Competition Winner

Jordan Windholz

psalm xxv

suppose the lungs unlatch
        like an ancient book, their narratives
loosed from the hermetic press

        of page upon page. suppose the story
they reveal resembles the anatomy
        of doves, the migratory patterns of certain

pacific starfish that court
        the currents around sandbars or coral. suppose
its subplots scatter letters and lines

        to gluts of consonance and assonance
once it's found out. or suppose the chest
        is a salt-worn residence, its planks

warped and gouged with pests, its floors
        littered with stories and songs. suppose one
of them speaks of exodus and genesis as stemming

from the same seed. imagine the tangle
as metaphor is made. outside the doors
　　　of books or home, in wilderness, imagine

a bush haloed by rose hips, gnarled with light,
　　　itself a conflation of burning and speaking.

—Nominated by the University of Colorado at Boulder

Alex Grant

The Steps of Montmartre

—after Brassai's 1936 photograph

On the steps of Sacre Coeur
        Cathedral, in that same winter
            when *junge leute* filled Bavarian

beer-gardens, ten years before
        Adorno proclaimed that there
            could be no art after Auschwitz,

Brassai captured his flawless
        image. Through the tunnel
            formed by the parting trees,

battalions of lamp-posts advance
        and retreat in the morning mizzle,
            clamp chain-link handrails hard

into sunwashed cobbles. In less
        than a year, the corpseless heads
            on Nanking's walls will coalesce

with Guernica's ruined heart, *mal*
    du siècle will become *Weltschmerz*,
        and the irresistible symmetry

of a million clacking boot heels
    will deafen half a continent.
        The red brush never dries—

adagio leads finally to fugue,
    haiku to satori, and the image
        fixed in silver to remembering.

—*Nominated by* Poemeleon: A Journal of Poetry

Benjamin Gotschall

Bait

When I found her, the ewe
still lived. Her head bloomed
from the place her face had been,
each breath red spume. Throat crushed,
tongue eaten, hind legs chewed
to bone, she made no sound
but a gurgle. I shot her

and dragged the body to where
tracks in snow found sand. Knelt
on a burlap sack, I hacked
frozen ground with a hatchet.
I opened the steel-jawed yawn, nocked
trigger to pan, sifted dry dirt
over top and smoothed it to look
like nothing. Nearby,

on shit flecked with bits of wool
I dripped piss milked
from a coyote bladder.
When I finished, the fat sun

squatted on a hilltop, then
slunk behind, silent. The trap,
nested in its bed, rested,
patient and certain as morning.

—Open Competition Winner

David Welch

Tribute

This wasn't the first time or the last,
wasn't the first time we thought of stone or the sparked and flushed light.

The flood was an afterthought of the river and the river of a greater crime.

This was when names were begotten with a polish of rainwater.

Names are that which we give to what we otherwise forget, which is why I don't work for
      memory.
That's one thing and not the other.

I do love your name—how, when I realize the windows are best left open, it rolls out like
      thunder.
The small flood on the sill, too, is an afterthought, but like the river it forgets to end up in
      our mouths.

Mouths that keep rivers under the tongue like rumor.

Mouths that sing tribute to storms.

And though it's not the first time, the sill swells in moist air.

And because I don't know the intricacies of a dovetail, it won't be the last, the last being
      a tribute to the labor of clouds in dry season.

This was when we first reclined in advancement.
This was when we skipped stones over tongues of the river.

     This was when.

In labor, a brief river precedes the child.

Through the radio, the siren hums out a rumor of flood.

It's a story I'd rather not tell.

—Open Competition Winner

Beth Bachmann

Nesting

Beneath the bridge, swallows mold the mask
of a woman's face,

clustering mud and tufts of hair dredged up
from a ditch,

leaving an interruption large enough to enter,
to spit wings,

which is an odd way to invoke annunciation,
a sudden blow.

The bones are narrow, so the birds take turns.
When it's over,

          the ground below whitens.

                —Open Competition Winner

Jee Leong Koh

Brother

In mother's womb, we started as a pair of lungs,
sea slugs hanging on to a reef. We grew toe rays,
brain sponges and gonads relaxed by the liquid song.

The *Doppler* ultrasound echoed our submarine
and found us one. The truth was monozygotic—
we sucked each other's nub of thumb inside the brine.

When, headfirst, we were unceremoniously expelled,
we were halved like an egg sliced with a line of hair.
A beak plucked at the cord and knotted my navel.

Mother never speaks of you although I know
you were with me at sea. How else to understand
my panic playing hide-and-seek, the cracked canoe,

wet dreams of touching a man, waking up, a curse
crying, not knowing why, like a turtle washed ashore,
a lacquered carapace—these shimmering absences?

—*Nominated by* The Ledge Magazine

Natalie Lyalin

Freak Inside the Heart

There were exquisite surgeons under lamplight,

there was a breeze before surgery.

Before surgery the doctors took notes.

I refused to speak with Satan, there

was really no need for that contact. The mound

was small, there were so many other cities,

three hundred years ago bells still rang, and now

a broken steam pipe by the cemetery. I said,

the city is a comfort. I said, check the fire exit.

I said, clear away the thicket of berries, the

mess hall rang with spoons, the clocks pointed

to the end of talking, there was really nothing

left to say. There was a sort of honesty in our

killing. It made the rest sit together. It made

the news deliver messages. It made history make

room for us. It bought flowers in lieu of flowers.

Then they reconsidered knitting. Reconsidered not

offering rides home. They took out the kaleidoscopes

and gemstones. They made one giant kaleidoscope

and felt like gentlemen. Like gentle men.

—Nominated by the University of Massachusetts

Natalie Diaz

Why I Don't Mention Flowers When Conversations with My Brother Reach Uncomfortable Silences

> *Forgive me, distant wars, for bringing flowers home.*
> —Wislawa Szymborska

In the Kashmir Mountains,
my brother shot many men,
blew skulls from brown skins,
dyed white desert sand crimson.

What is there to say to a man
who has traversed such a world,
whose hands and eyes have
betrayed him?

Were there flowers there? I asked.

This is what he told me:

In a village, many men
wrapped a woman in a sheet.

She didn't struggle.
Her bare feet dragged in the dirt.

They laid her in the road
and stoned her.

The first man was her father.
He threw two stones in a row.
Her brother had filled his pockets
with stones on the way there.

The crowd was a hive
of disturbed bees. The volley
of stones against her body
drowned out her moans.

Blood burst through the sheet
like a patch of violets,
a hundred roses in bloom.

—Open Competition Winner

JoAnn Balingit

History Textbook, America

I'd search for Philippines in History class.
The index named one page, moved on to Pierce.
The Making of America marched past
my enigmatic father's place of birth.
The week he died some man we didn't know
called up. *This is his brother,* one more shock,
phoning for him. "He died three days ago."
The leaden black receiver did not talk.
My uncle never gave his name or town,
we never heard from him. Was it a dream?
The earpiece roar dissolved to crackling sounds,
a dial tone erased the Philippines.
And yet my world grows huge with maps, crisscrossed,
my History alive with all I've lost.

—Open Competition Winner

Greta Wrolstad

Notes on Sea and Shore

As for gold's effect on the first white men
on this continent, a Nahuatlan scribe said *they
fingered it as if their hearts were illumined
and made new.* Let us return to the explorer's
magazine, its pages of ocean awash in gold-and-
more-gold, that warm hued metal stable
in the sea's salinity and stable in air. When
the dead men appeared dressed in golden

fish scales, radiating through the dark, how warm their
metal light was, how much more
steady than that on the river seen
daily through our windows: amber-lit buoys
blinking atop black water. Let us return
to that time when we loved nothing more
than the photographs of sunken galleons,
their rapid decline in an inverted world.

You were in your room overlooking the bay
and never once glanced at the water, stayed
with the blinds drawn, waited in the crowded
rooms of your skull for the tide to rise.
And it was at that time I was learning
the names of southern trees, saying *jacaranda,*
pohutakawa as their tangled shapes slid by
the windshield. On every street I drove

the same trees loomed overhead, at every turn—
the ocean. I agree with the man who said *being*
in a ship is being in a jail with
the chance of drowning. I stay on the
shore, the bay's flat crown obscuring
its depth. Here starfish divide and grow
anew, amass on the rocks, their spiny rays
fingering the tide's ever-loosening border.

And the stones gather to be unraveled. Gulls nest
high above the waterline suckling the shore.
Do you know the common rate of fall
for any weight pitched over the edge?
The common descent, that *human bone*
consists of an animal and an earthly part
intimately bound together—how sad
it must be, shackled. If only there were

an edge to that edge—but each confluence is
tethered to foreign parts, rushes on, a thirty-three-
point-three percent animal frothing itself
out of itself, breaking those bonds
through stubborn movement. The physicians
discovered that in bones Haversian canals
run parallel for a while, then branch
and communicate. What end do we seek.

Forget this northern shore: cold and colder
by the day, an owl inking the night with its throat.
When I sleep I see a man with seeds
stuffed in his pockets, seeds bundled in wet
gauze. He paddles the Strait of Malacca,
to a lush shore lined with magnolias (I imagine
the scene incorrectly), their velvet flowers
thickening the sand's edge, weighed down

by scent. When I awaken, I row out to the
barrier island where a woman dressed in blue
once lived in a wooden house silvered by
the sea. Suspended in the attic:
a wooden trapeze, softened by the hands of
dangling children. The house is gone,
the island without a single owl's nest.
Forgive me, I have forgotten myself.

To be sailing the Sargasso Sea, where life is *caught and held indefinitely*...no wind nor currents to carry matter away. Day-after-day lie afloat on a shoreless sea, a sea clogged with kelp, felled kelp, fallen upwards to air and collected there by a hurricane's pull. Our warm bodies bobbing bloodless on the brown ocean, strong and steady,

oblivious to this ebb tide—shielded by the Sargasso Sea caught and held by our own two hands, caught and held. Still clinging to Floridian rocks, West Indian rocks, dross smeared across the mid-Atlantic. Everything suspends in a final suspension; everything linked and floating, as a left hand takes the right to keep it warm.

Once again I am huddled under the freighted
ocean, where memory is swallowed by
the dark recesses, the descending aorta of our
common form: a form the anatomy
book says is of *small size and
imperfect development at birth*. For months
I have wanted to send you a drawing,
exceedingly detailed, showing ourselves without

skin. Imagine you received it. Imagine you are
the page which water has never touched.
How quickly this all lapses into imperfection.
I have heard that under all liquid is the shape
that we are seeking, a landscape
where we do not descend with time,
but drift through the throat's murky
catacombs, weightless in a silken interior.

Silently lying in the margins, sheltering as the North Shore's ferry terminal with its wide eaves: a note (in lovely penmanship) says on August 24, 1961, at Point-No-Point the sea was edged in *Ralfsia pacifica,* commonly known as the Tar Spot, undreamable seaweed seeming to be oil. The spots recur every spring, emerging whole once again from winter's paring, and

what I would give to know such growth, such sure formless growth, but no trail returns to Point-No-Point, not even your notes accurately track that rain-drenched shoreline—where surely, the rain must never cease—that shoreline arcing from crag to crag, piles of stone thickening. And the only shelter left is a trace of your left hand curled around the pen, holding as it moved.

And the sole shelter left is a scrawl in the book
about men traversing the Pacific, searching
for the Southern Continent, for proof of
balance on this earth. It must have been
an awful voyage: the water, only the slosh of
water for months. When land appeared it was
inhabited by men gnawing on the
remains of other men. A dead woman

floating in the cove. The explorers did not
stay. Facing oddly away from the direction
they moved towards, as if with *eyes at
the back of their heads,* they rowed from
the beach where a shot man lay flat
on his back, holding a bolt of cloth.
No continent was found. Underneath,
water complicated the ship's wooden form.

Will this motion ever quiet. Everything incessantly oscillating, as if all life is *that rocking life imparted by a gently rolling ship* and lacking a stable bearing. Yet this is no terror. Only a lullaby from which the danger is waking. Suppose we are all unmoored. Suppose we are all tethered to the high rigging of our own ship-mast in mid-ocean, on duty to look ever outward,

navigating by horizon. In our throats a strange thirst persists. Perhaps there would be an end. Comes a shoreline. Comes a harbor—a river. *And our identities come back in horror* at the river's mouth that pleads for more silt, more sand, refuses to slide clean to the sea. At the river's first bend we come ashore, and on that shore, stones. Smooth, diminishing stones.

—*Nominated by* Black Warrior Review

Rebecca Wadlinger

Pet Fungus in Our Zoo Rehearsing the National Requiem

> *—title of an Icelandic science experiment in which crickets in three adjacent chambers were simultaneously exposed to constant low-sinus audio, electromagnetic fields, and ultraviolet light*

The National Museum of Monday
is closed on Mondays. *Ad Honorem.*

In the aquarium, pet fungus rehearses
the national requiem. You sleep in.

You dream you're a surgeon;
your mother awakens on the table

& in front of all the pretty nurses
she grabs your scalpel & wags it at you

scolding Don't you dare mention my
"appendectomy." Your medical test asked

Heart? & you answered C, a chambered
gun that explodes inadvertently.

Even the appendectomy is closed
on Mondays. Rehearse, in your glass

house, a requiem for the final Monday—
beneath your ribs, that automatic

dreaming. You are adding an appendix
to the list of Monday's closures:

the melodies of eukaryotes, it begins,
the instrumental ache of decomposers.

—Nominated by The University of Texas

K.A. Hays

Serotinous

We should learn from them: the copse
of pitch pines leaning into a mohawk, all needle
and warted twig. If someone lit a blaze

out here, they wouldn't blink; they have,
in fact, grown dormant buds made

to open in such terror. Good idea for us
to fashion, like them, root collars—so if the body
cooked to the nub, buds gone, another self

might climb out, cough, unfold greenly—
though safer still, for the populace, to be schooled

in serotinous cones, to learn to lock our seed
in a resin that melts off only in fire
so if the bud and root and trunk are cooked,

the seeds are saved, and spring from the charred earth
after the dumb maples and oaks, with their studied

aesthetics of leaf and even shade, samaras
and acorns, have gone. The pitch pines welter,
clawed on ledges with their roots in near-rock,

fed by the ground's toxic metals. Remember—
if not for the arbitrary crash that startled off

a piece of the planet, forming the moon and tilting
the earth off-kilter, there would be no us. How dull
that would be, the hardier insects moping about

without our drama, limp and uninspired, no religion
or politics to stir the blood. Convenient

that we have this creator latent in us,
erratic, poised to start a burn.

—*Nominated by* Black Warrior Review

Julie Sophia Paegle

Clock & Echo

Confession is the better communion—

no stale wafer disintegrating
        to the palate and sticking, flattened barnacle dying down
    the throat, there stung with acid wine—

    I'll take the tight body of wood

anointing my sins anytime: echo beginning.   My own words
    muffled, made familiar, made sound & sin & part
of the marble that makes cathedral dome

    hold sky—what oiled wood can do to words!

What snow falling can do to morning   what space in a bed can do to *recline*.

    Some time before this morning

we lay in the aftermath of our overture.
    There was a fire.   The strings inside the piano still

hummed. Coffin box with harp & keys by a fire. Or a restored
      grandfather clock, its missing pendulum swing-dancing the air. Your flush like
a woman. You loved that you were more beautiful than I. Well, you too would have

grown old—still, we did establish an

      intimacy. You knew what there is
          to know of my body, where skin stretches & where skin lies.
You were remarkably here
      in the important moments of the body.
& you thought, *you* thought!—the priests could still be shocked. So we would try.

      So to St. John. So to the Divine. So I miss that a building

can hold so much sky—all that rock rising
               just to bring some space inside—& here is

what I know of this morning: snow is falling in sheaths & columns. Hidden
      priests are always becoming
beautiful. The sun is distant & the temperature is falling. Soon the snow
      will fall in crystals & pile on the leaves piled on the lawn & soon some
priest will welcome our desire & his shock will always be sublime. Soon the days
will shift down the hours, obscuring the evening & lighting the dawn & soon there
will be no need to write of priests or leaf piles since very soon now I will
      write, *now that you are gone—*

—*Nominated by* The Cream City Review

Morgan Lucas Schuldt

Triptych for Francis Bacon

> *I am always hoping to deform people into appearance...*
> —Francis Bacon

If shape is a finished thing, what is this? A black background, a few white verticals, a few horizontals lending depth to a darkness. A convergence of lines suggesting the corners of a transparent box. The tentative outlines of a showcase, or a glass cell. Or else a room of some kind—the steep tilt of a floor meeting a wall, the wall a low ceiling. Lines that, in their faint drag across the canvas, confine a darkness, and in that darkness the hunkered clump of something human. Bald gore of the un-rinsed under-life. A hunch in a suit or a mouth with a tie. Interrogator? Lover? Pontiff? Something insubstantial. Isolated. A waiting figure blur-bound and boxed-up. Adumbrated but alone. Hardly differentiated from its surrounding space. At no point let to fulfill itself. Everything below the waist open-ended, continuous. Neither elegant nor useful—its sex indistinguishable from a wall. Untouchable. Fleshless. An idea given up on.

Better than memory, better even than love, & more dependable—anger, which ignores the long *because* and, instead, simplifies, ignores. As dear Peter in Tangiers. The gin-tinged temper. Their brawl. Thirty or so canvases gashed-gone, cast to the cobble below. The abrupt blood on the floor, the rest swallowed. Past gathering, past putting back—an inspiration.

~

Your imagination—a room. A butcher's stall where the 19th century is taken by surprise. Cleaved with a brush, semblance skinned and splayed. Or hung from a hook and dangled to drip—the raw haunch of perspective. Because love for you means carcass. Means fresh violence and anything beyond repair. Anything rubbed raw and un-relievable. Flanks sloughed in a bed. Mouths vaguely human, biting at empty air. Stuck open as if to remind us there is no certainty between pleasure and pain. A scumble. A gouge. Meaty shades of red and blue. The absolute afterall: bare flesh & the wound—where the living, the dying is done.

—Nominated by Sentence

Dora Malech

A Shortcut

A hedgehog shuffles out to take a moment
of the moon. The moon leaves off trying on
cloud after cloud to render for a moment
the frowsy foliage and the nose beneath
in tenebrous strokes, not light and dark,
but light in dark or light in spite of.
Doesn't rinse the brush to touch the lilies'
brief white swash and sticky spots
of seeds and pulp where the karakas bend
and drop their drupes. Sprays of stone-fruit
come to sweet rot underfoot with a stench
that in a warmer, brighter hour would draw
the flies to feed at each smear adhered, here
to the asphalt switchback and there to the stairs
that teeter through the terraces and past
the walls that prop the city up above the sea,
walls studded with snails after a day of rain.
The young snails resemble pearl barley, pale,
scattered as at some strange matrimony,
the old are dark burls grown somehow from brick.
Egalitarian spectrum renders the memory

of the sun's gaudy palette obsolete
here where each edge is a glint and each
hollow, a shadow. Holds at first glance each
as distant and as dear, though an eye that waits
to warm to, lets its iris open into
finds that though both take a glimmer, the shell
knows one way to shine and the body, another.
The former's luster, a crystal ball in which
one sees the muddy future, the latter,
a small brown tongue pronouncing "like" against
a concrete palate, careful. Only the wind hurries
here, and the leaves turn aside to let it pass,
shake disapproval. A spider rests
after mending its nets, sits at the center
of tenuous nebula wound from catkin
to fern frond to the black beaks of the last flax,
an almost-still-life. Here a twitch and there
a shiver and each snail's nacreous wake
belies if not progress then process,
illuminated glyphs, transient text, a glisten
spelling if not here-to-there then
somewhere-to-somewhere
by way of these walls that hold the hills from
their someday certain spill into the harbor
a moment more and then another moment
more for each of our small sakes.

—*Open Competition Winner*

Tyler Mills

Violin Shop

Instruments hang from the ceiling,
stiff necks, bodies burnished gold,
curved like pheasants, mute swans, a rare condor,
so valuable that symphony musicians
borrow these forms only for specific concerts,
such as *Scheherazade,* where a violin solo
draws the hushed audience
inside itself like rows of oars
sliding on the flat deck of a Phoenician ship.
In the shop, luthiers worry—they wipe
varnish on their apron pockets.
Glass pots gleam yellow with boiled glue,
and slips of tan horsehair fan the worktables;
the silver tools small enough to fit inside my mouth
cannot make *Guarneri del Gesu* speak.
Rumors say the three-hundred-year-old
violin hid beneath the bed of a man in Spain
while a bullet spat his wet blood:
a clean red arc across the floor. Black *f* slits
angle in an "antagonistic" way—the violin mutters,
complains under the chin of Berlin

Philharmonic musicians. I read this
in the *Chicago Tribune*. The shop owners
stood over the wood instrument, praying
for its voice, they brewed coffee,
rubbed its body with swatches of velvet,
then they called a man, an exorcist,
who probably laid the violin
down on the stock market page
as if it was a pumpkin, round,
hairy inside with seed-pulp, and chanted,
hollowing out its cavity: the voice that laughed at Bach,
groaned through Tchaikovsky's concerto
that usually runs so fast trees blur,
that spoke out loud longer than you
or I ever will and wanted to comment
finally on how things really are, was cured.

—*Nominated by* Indiana Review

Erin M. Bertram

[Mesmerist]

Find me fractured, head on one shoulder like a colt,

composure just one more heady illusion. An apple beneath
my top hat to remember the weight of sin, cape tied

too tight for austerity's sake—a showman's finely taut face.

If, sleight of hand, quick flick of the wrist, a gesture fails
to impress, what—abrupt? meticulous?—move next to call my own?

Slats comprise the box, 2 x 4's just for show. Evenings

I saw her in half, mornings she expects reassembly

with a steady hand. So I acquiesce, spent of tricks
from the night before. What appears magic (materialization,

complete & total dismissal) so many lights, pipe smoke,

one more card tucked neatly up the sleeve. When I meet
my face in the glass, rouge smeared, gloves sawdust

sallow, I am the lion's mane, I am the vanishing dove.

—Open Competition Winner

Kristin Kelly

Endings

You are told you have two choices: wreck or
get off the train. You dress in black

either way. You consider a parasol,
light luggage for the latter, polka dots.

You want to be brief but loud, spotted
in the crowd, especially if it is raining,

you want a stranger with paints to want
to paint you, to say *stop there, bright thing, be still.*

But if you wreck, you pack it all—
boots, bitters, the letter most hard to read. You go

unperfumed, touching the backs of chairs,
even the emptied, *saying thanks, no thank you,*

duck, duck, goose. There will be a long chase,
an even longer sex scene. Each involves high

heels, and both times you get caught. *Get off,*
they tell you, *last hoorah.* But a man

stays on, chewing mints. He has his own
couchette and two pillows, one for either side

of his head. You have your rhyme, your reason,
a borrowed sleeping bag, that photograph and,

because it is between seasons, a swimsuit
and some firewood. Where to, he asks,

and you want to. But the rain, the whistle,
the black spots of cattle, the spark of foil under a chair,

the fingerprints bare and flowering on the window—
they keep you. They keep you still.

—Open Competition Winner

C. Wade Bentley

Fortune

Cesar the gay Guatemalan and Mai Anh the Vietnamese refugee
arrived at my office together and not only occupied the two wooden
chairs I've placed there for students but seemed to fill my entire office
in much the same way fragrance from a couple of *carne asada*
streetcarts can blanket a city block.

Cesar's the talker—and, okay, the snappy dresser—swinging wildly
from passion (abusive father, sister in a coma) to passion (silk ties),
the one with fourteen new dreams for getting rich, who reminds his American
Government teacher *civilization* (saying the word in his head, first,
working the Spanish out of it) did *not* begin in North America.

Both students of mine a year or so back, since then they have
visited, together or separately, as regular as therapy—I don't know
why and have never asked their reasons, not wanting to intimate
that they shouldn't, that there is anything inappropriate, *not done*
about it, this post-class co-dependence.

Mai Anh, quieter, struggles with the language, sentences exploding
in expressive bits like ketchup pounded from a bottle, which is how,
with patience, you will learn that she escaped to Indonesia one night

with a hundred children on a small boat but thought all alone about pirates
and death and stars:

"... and felt that there was something good for me in the future,"
as she once wrote for my class but refused to read aloud. I have saved
the fortune cookies from a week of Chinese take-out (though Mai insists
I should let her cook me some *real* eggrolls) so today, as always, we haphazardly
choose, break them open, and laugh at how each one is true.

—Open Competition Winner

Chelsea Jennings

Landing

> *Some people said that when a Negro died he went back to Africa,*
> *but this is a lie. How could a dead man go to Africa? It was living*
> *men who flew there, from a tribe the Spanish stopped importing as*
> *slaves because so many of them flew away that it was bad for*
> *business.*
>   —Esteban Montejo, *The Autobiography of a Runaway Slave*

A field of scythes upright, a crop of arms in flight
too far from land—Uncanny
But I'll be damned if it wasn't even stranger
on the other side of things

*

The rivulets of ocean-salt on their shoulders
must have looked like feathers by the time
they touched down any-which-where

*

Their palms were angled against the air
to slow down, graceful as takeoff
But they had little in the way of examples
for landing—

They twisted ankles and suffered concussions
and could hardly raise their arms for days

*

(Soon the sheep got used to them lying there
and went back to conjuring grass from the ground)

*

When the flock of them finally walked into town
ghosted over with dust, the soles of their feet
brown as blood, they were told:

    We've long since finished our ritual grief
    If you come back again, you better really be dead

—Open Competition Winner

Elizabeth Langemak

A Brief History of Sainthood

When the first, still just a woman, looked up

into loving she knew she must reach down

      for better pains: reach with her arms,

their lengths already veined with scars, strain

with splinter-wedged nails and gnawed

      fingers, stretch her guts and ass and hook

her anchor in something deep because

suffering is our only biography and

      not all are written. Pinprick, back-lash, stones

in her pockets: there was light at the end

of each wound, God at the bottom of lakes

      as she sunk, God again in the breath

as she surfaced. If she could not walk

on water, the least she could do was nearly

      drown. This was her greatest discovery:

air from lungs, blood from vein, bone out

      of socket, child expelled from the womb

and then broken by words that refuse

      to come back, by slow separation.

Or quick. The trick was in the healing: scabs,

      the sets, the body a pigeon returned

to itself on holier wings, frail but alive

with a message hung in its beak: *I will tear*

      you apart. Tear yourself first.

                  —*Open Competition Winner*

Elizabeth Knapp

Betray

It began not
with a kiss of fury, the dark heavens opening
     like labial folds to swallow Him complete,
          whole, while Judas wept
     in the shadows, fingering his promise
          of gold, the pouch he
               would kill or die for—

     One of you
will betray me. No. It began with a kiss of indifference.
     In the night, a single hibiscus bloom
          unfolded despite me, despite
     whatever storm would later
          ravage it, despite my refusal
               to water it, ignoring

     its scarlet profusion,
its gaudy announcement of resistance.
     Two days later, I knew, it would be gone.
          Who can say with certainty

what Judas felt, as he lingered
    in the garden after they
        had taken Him away,

the tin shield
of the moon now polished and risen, the silver
    knives of the olive trees glinting, the stones
        now dumb and cold? No one cares
about Judas's own dark night of the soul,
    as he slept on the bones
        of his savior. I will

betray every flower
that opens for me, praying not for indifference—
    the kiss of a wind that would flatten them
        in caprice, or a frost that would ice
their tongues as they fold back to the dust
    of my making—pray they die not in spite
        but because of me.

—*Open Competition Winner*

Todd Hearon

In the Garden

Alzheimer's Ward, Eden Gardens, Rock Hill, South Carolina

Tonight the memory I want, beyond my own,
is all my father's now. Tonight the memory
I want is what he calls his *first,* his *all alone,*

his mother, in a window with the sun
falling through the leaves of a pecan,
singing "In the Garden" as she irons . . .

There is a music, far back in the mind,
that falls like light through a gap in the garden fence
and climbs the waist-high thistles, dandelions

and almost, almost touches where I stand
outside that window with its host of shadows,
bottle-full of clipped perennials and cooling iron.

—*Nominated by* Harvard Review

Christi Kramer

Biography of awe

Bray, the roof of the mouth, donkey's unbroken back,

Each day, she prepares for the end of the world; sweeps, waters the parsley, folds
the photo into the cloth.

Each day he swings a leg over and is thrown off again, the donkey
each day runs leaping to the well.

The stake is pulled out, a fist or bullet enters, breath rubs against rib.

The new word for love, for pain, for beauty, he whispers in the donkey's ear.
Realization, the vista, this amount. A huge, horrible world colliding.

Once there was a judge here who ladled justice hot into the hands.
Once he put his own head in his hands, laid his head down.

And for the new weight and rocking, for the bridal bed,
for the breaking, there is this word.

—*Nominated by* PRACTICE: NEW WRITING + ART

Craig Blais

Sister at the Airport

On my sister's nights off, she takes the train to the airport and haunts the security gates.
While man, woman, and child wait in line for random screenings, she stands to the side,
    with the other families,
Waiting for loved ones to arrive, weary, and smiling, from the other side of the exit
    doors.
My sister tells me that Milwaukee is all cheap beer and good-byes; she prefers to be in a
    place where

People arrive. She tells me, with no sense of shame, that the degree of pleasure she feels
    is contingent
On sex, age, race, and perceived social standing. While my sister feels little for the
    middle-class
Mother fingering her key ring and car alarm remote in expectation of her son—coming
    home
From some private university in the South—she's moved to tears at the sight of a child
Holding a cardboard sign that reads *WELCOME HOME DADDY.*

My sister has conversations with those standing in wait. No feeling, she says, is so strong
    or pure
As the anticipation of reunion. She listens to their stories and fills with their excitement,

Or else excuses herself to go buy coffee. Sometimes my sister tells them she is waiting
    for her boyfriend:
Coming home "on leave." Other times, if she doesn't feel like talking, she is there
To pick up her housemate, heading back from a business trip. And sometimes

She is there to greet me, her brother, returning from someplace far off. When we were
    younger,
She was often responsible for retrieving me from the airport. It was always late at night
And everybody else had become bored with homecomings. I am afraid that's when this
    all started.
The whole way home, she could only speak of the people she waited with; as we drove
Past the penitentiary, and the fox standing alone in the field of snow beside it, she would
    go on and on.

—Nominated by Wichita State University

Christina Duhig

What Places, Things

A drink of something. Not tea, sky. You ask for the sky
In a shade of purple. A pickup truck and I, you say I

Must write the particulars. A certain word, at least one
Time, all sand and aster. And I ask what. We make us

With these things. Between here and Ohio. Not the sky,
Your pickup. Purple then, a thin thread. Laced to the town

We fled with CB radios. It's me. Two blocks from the East
River, a man curses in Polish and sleeps. Splintered chairs

And box spring, a broken-down Toyota where a house
Should stand. Once I crept close enough to touch the water-

Stained upholstery, but wrote you instead. Once you called
Just to read me a poem. The poem begins with margaritas,

A man in New York and a woman. In Virginia, it ends
With stars. Something about earrings, grapes. The color

Over the river. Just before the sun slips, it's you. I always
Answer. Revise the love story, where. A lake skirts

The places we paint, thirsty and orange. This is how we know
The other. We hedge our bets with the sky. We call it geography.

—Open Competition Winner

Scott Glassman

Drinks over the Medusa Fossae

I come to you as a detail
of slopes between the highlands
and lowlands, straddling
Tharsis and Elysium—

sky, a declivity
of ash.

The water-bearing
inner channels I remember of you,
visible still.

Before the deposition,
the magenta of magma
flows, a blanket
spread over this plateau

hyacinths rippling
in a moonlit fissure,
what the moon
that night was made of.

—Nominated by Web del Sol

Margaret Ronda

Walking Late

Then up ahead, the man with the blue shirt. Follow me he said. The pink camellias
glared flat-eyed. Car after car passing, tinny red taillights.

How many bones in the body. There was a line drawn through it.

Circuitry of paths, one meant *to lie*. Then we were abandoned by lawns, and concrete sprang
up in meadows. He said stay close. I could smell his skin.

Ribcage pushed against the hand.

Hastening now, and sometimes a boy running out a back door. Or a cloud pulling apart
above us. I left a trail of silver rings hanging on branches.

A nest threaded, a maze. And how to say hold back, hold.

I see the hills he said. How they've split you open. Night by now, kids setting off fireworks
down the street. Half-circles of sparks, then black.

A sound like the subway coming. And what voice said leap.

—Nominated by The Eleventh Muse

Kara Candito

Carnivale, 1934

Burlesque Dancer

Tell me about the Badlands,
     where we hid in the dry riverbed
and whispered *deluge* until our breath filled
     the cracked cups. How it was dark
when we dug up the baby and wrapped him
     like a little papoose again.

It wasn't like headlights, the seams
     they left on the side of the road.
It was more like the dotted lines I drew down
     my sister's calves where stockings
belonged. How it was hot in the tent
     and we put peacock feathers

in our hair and danced until we forgot
     the mans' hands in the matinee.
How we swore we'd drive out to Los Angeles
     where the fog unzips its white dress,
and I'd learn to dance like Shirley Temple.
     Smile and slap my dimples.

Look at the girl splayed out on the dusty stage.
      Look at the stars, at Orion unbuckling
himself. That means we're in Cheyenne,
      that means we'll never see the coast.
Tell me the things you say to yourself
      when there are stray dogs
                at the edge
                    of every town.

—*Nominated by Florida State University*

Kelly Madigan Erlandson

Reliquary

Always I am taking the wounded from the mouth of the hungry,
the wet fur of the leveret from the jaws of the hound.

Or I am the one with the sledgehammer, the poisoned steak
that I slip over the fence after every authority refused
to quarantine the beast. I have to protect my own,

        but the world assigns too many to me,
says they are each my own, the lobsters in the tank
at the market, the sparrows in the neighbor's trap,
the massive tawniness at the edge of the field at dusk.

        I love the world that wants to eat me,
and I crave to devour it, too—smear my face with butter and grease,
talk into the night about meals I've had.

        I am the paralyzed rescuer,
watching the nest mown over, waving from the porch
as the men head off with their long guns. If I have been sent here
for some task, I have blundered, I have failed.
I couldn't find the trap door, the men with the proper authority.

Yet I rest my feet in the stream and it washes me anyway,
and birds make nests of ribbons in my eaves. I am sorry. I was ill
equipped. I can't even tell you I will do better.

But I will collect the bones, I will stand
at the roadside and say your names, *Porcupine, Mule Deer, Wildcat.*
I will take what lasts longest, the jaw bone set with jewels,
let it bleach in the white heat.

I will say I knew you, that I found it by Salt Creek,
or in the Big Horns. I will show the architecture of your mouth
to children. I will let them run their fingertips, whorled with identity,
over the tops of your marvelous teeth.

—Open Competition Winner

Jamie Ross

Peterbilt

So he falls again. And again. From the bed, the
stairs, his low-slung chair, my father, from my fable. As
night falls, I fall, as snow falls on the cabin, on routes
these years have cut in rock, the clutch, the scar
that wraps his forearm tighter to the wheel, turning
asphalt into dawn or dusk, the darkness
of a certain skin whose yearning spreads like fire. He's
driving wind now pressed against each stud, each
bolt and rivet in the gray ravines above the Mancos
pounding slate and rotten schist, sunken willow,
driving up the banks, the piling vaults, packing
freight in sleet, in seeking rain, each light
obscured by flesh, the red star route of backrow
streets, the black side-roll through Hatch, he's
driving grease the spitfire pots
the dirty coffee counter smears of more or don't
until the gears heat harder, higher up the Cumbres passage
into pine and sheet-bent poplar breaking back
beyond the throat of gasoline through grinding valves the glassy
skin near sudden bone of stare through father driving
blood twelve tons of sheep four tiers of panic bleating

shit my father drive me drive this son I push
against this stench the speed the gun-gray bales, against this box
behind the cab, the bed behind us farther farther throttled
beachhead splitcraft pylons crumbling steeper metal twisted
hands her face above the silos, fields, roast-pit red, pushed to
pavement, pistons, driving snow, driving bridge, the diving like-
ness of yourself when the child came down in the mist of names.

—*Nominated by* Northwest Review

Catherine Pierce

Epithalamium

First, know the type of car the other drove
as a high school senior, late eighties. Were there
bucket seats? Red interior? You must love
that car. You must wish, at least briefly, that you
had ridden in it. Next, you must understand
the psychology of the belt buckle and the black boots.
They were chosen for a reason. Know that reason
and never speak of it. Purchase for each other
not only books and dinners, but plastic
serving trays, origami kits, a postcard from Tupelo
to be hand-delivered, unmarked. Be kind to old
photographs, but not overly kind. Know the name
of a town in Mexico where you can someday,
money willing, spend a week. Consider starting
a four-piece cover band. Consider growing
basil and/or marijuana. Know that at no point
do you have to own a) tapered jeans, b) a good blender,
c) spare light bulbs. These are your decisions to make.
Remember small parts of many days: the Amish

restaurant outside the city. The purchase of the red vase.
The bird whose cries woke you your first morning
in one bed. How you rose together then.

—*Open Competition Winner*

Michelle McEwen

Blood

There is always a leader amongst them—
the girl-cousins. She is the one who is allowed
to sit at the table with the aunts-mothers-wives—
trusted with the big knife when it comes time
to slice the watermelon. She is the one
who bleeds first. The one the aunts talk
about in smile-heavy whispers: they say
she will be knocked-up before she knows it,
before *that* chapter is even gotten 'round
to in health class. It is she who makes
her boy-cousins wish blood wasn't as thick
as all that.

In vacation photos, she smiles the hardest—
hands on hips, head to one side, hair hanging;
hickies trophy-shiny in the sun. She is the one
who makes out with the local kid before
the trip ends. And when she promises to keep
in touch, you can almost see the bolding-&-italicizing
of her "I will"s and "I swear"s.

The aunts try not to smile when they say
that girl is going to mess around and get
killed by some man one of these days. She is
the one who notices, first, the fresh blood
staining your bikini bottom. Taking you by the hand,
she drags you out from the water, leads you
to the ladies' room as though you are not the same
age as her, as though she is already somebody's
mother.

—*Open Competition Winner*

Elyse Fenton

Gratitude

Wreckage was still smoldering on the airport road
when they delivered the soldier—*beyond recognition,*

seeing god's hands in the medevac's spun rotors—
to the station's gravel landing pad. By the time you arrived

there were already hands fluttering white flags of gauze
against the ruptured scaffolding of ribs, the glistening skull, and no skin

left untended, so you were the one to sink the rubber catheter tube.
When you tell me this over the phone hours later I can hear rotors

scalping the tarmac-gray sky, the burdenless lift of your voice.
And I love you more for holding the last good flesh

of that soldier's cock in your hands, for startling his warm blood
back to life. Listen. I know the way the struck chord begins

to shudder, fierce heat rising into the skin of my own
sensate palms; that moment just before we think

the end will never come and then
the moment when it does.

—Nominated by University of Oregon

Donika Ross

Ceremony

He wrenches the meat from bone
with forefinger and thumb, and the whitened
muscle mounds the kitchen table. Through
the window, grackles code themselves

on clotheslines and along the ridge of sheds—
clumps and voids that seem to read *His wife
was a dancer. He is inconsolable.* Outside,
he loosens the birds, buries the meat

below his drying shirts. He lets the dirt clot
and dry his grease slicked fingers. The birds
return, and he is just a man, still, altering
rocks at the lip of a filled hole.

—Nominated by the University of Texas

Brett Foster

The First Request of Lazarus

1.

> *...so newly separated*
> *From the old fire of Heaven.*
> —Ovid

Already weary
from second living, new
dying of renewed patience,

old Lazarus of Bethany
betrays the uplift, desperate
for a death pregnant

with meaning, reliable passing.
How does one return,
happily, to work the olive groves?

How to age now? Even feasts
felt nebulous, and villages—
he seemed beyond them. True,

nothing terrifies like that
desertion: fading one
swallowed in the cave mouth,

linen strips to bind
the limbs. Though loss like this,
however uniquely it strikes

the forsaken, is ordinary still,
more familiar than altars,
fruitful as peasant markets.

2.

> *...there is nothing*
> *But howling wind and solitary birds.*
> —William Butler Yeats

This Lazarus, body rich
with sickness, deathbed-ridden,
spoke of spent candles,

tabernacles, frankincense.
Dogs licked his sores.
His suffering justified

the rage, his matted beard,
the pure fear. Ah, the tomb's
thick silence: its air balmed

his aches like lanolin. Those days
undenied, then the honor—
a *rabbi's* tears as he bid

the boulder gone. He staggered
toward the stone aperture,
face wrapped in canvas.

Sisters could not barter grief
so quickly. Younger ones were called,
their return more painful.

They also know desire:
daughter of the synagogue ruler,
the widow's son at Nain.

3.
> *Changed from glory into glory,*
> *Till in heaven we take our place...*
> —Charles Wesley

As for him, he waits—
impatient, stone-jawed, face hanging
like spoiled fish. He gainsays

symbolism. He knows at last
we are destined for this,
we serve one purpose, fatally,

make good on this clay-made
existence only in keeping
our good, last word.

Ether, end breath. Mindless
derelictions near soliloquy, twice
uttered. Truth is less beautiful

in rehearsal. This vocation
serves an instant, laid for everyone.
Then, only then, would the earth

surrender its mortal turning,
open wide the oceans
to let its inhabitants pass,

carrying clumsy dynasties,
their destinations somewhere
otherwise, and not here.

—Nominated by I M A G E

Ed Madden

Sacrifice

When my father bound me, I submitted,

closed my eyes to the lifted knife in his fist.
Even now, the cords still hold my wrists,

rough ropes of love. My chest is bare,
my heart lies open. He loves his god more

than me. I open my eyes, watch my father
raise his fist against a bright and bitter

sky, no angel there to stay his hand.

—*Open Competition Prize Winner*

Tomas Q. Morin

At Klack's, 1941

for Son House

At the counter a finger taps
the pink jar of pig feet
and the thin brine jumps.
Outside, the Delta is flooding
with the shrills of twilight.
Down a grassy spur the iron
ring of a box car train thunders
wadded cotton to the crumbling
beds of the lower Midwest.

All along the river men
are busy disappearing
into the overgrowth. Tomorrow
they will return and stoop
again as one many-handed body
and spade the wet earth apart,
bank it against itself
to the rhythm of one
churning voice calling

and answering: *When I get*
back home, back home,
I'm gonna walk and tell,
that Mississippi river
is a burnin' hell.

Long into the hot dark, House
plays bare of chest, of head,
stomping hymns and psalms
he had pounded blue
in his heel day after day
while scratching the earth
on a tractor. That night
he made the music bleed
into the evening sounds,
showed why he left the pulpit
for the divine voice
in the steel bones of his guitar,
how he could still make it wail
and holler to the down-trodden
citizens of a godless hell.

—Open Competition Winner

Lyrics are adapted from a traditional work song.

Robert Sawyer

How I Know She's Coming Home

—for Jodi Lister

Her apricot soap French milled and expensive
Is wrapped in violet tissue paper
And hidden in the medicine cabinet.
In the dish on the sink she left behind
A bar of Ivory.

Plain and substantial as a baseball
That's for me.
Five thousand miles away
And she does not want me to use her soap.

I unwrap it and hold it as carefully
As an antique netsuke. Its perfume
Rises like a summer morning
Reaching through a screen door.

When she's here I receive strict instruction
Not to use her creams, shampoos or powders.
Although I may touch any part of her body I please
Her beauty products are taboo.

Yesterday, it removed bus exhaust and sweat
Leaving her face soft and damp,
So when I kissed her it was like touching moss.

Today, I run water, make a lather and inhale.
Although it's my face that looks back from the mirror
It is her scent that slips into the room
Like a secret hushed from the lips that held it.

—Open Competition Winner

Sarah Perrier

Pitch the Woo

Let's lose it, baby; let's forget
the fever, the flowers, the dinner and dancing
and all the jazzy lines we throw out for waiters

so they know they can slap that check down
anywhere they please. Give me your heart

on a platter. And look, your lovely, loose fist
opens to show off—like magic—mine. It's smaller
than you thought, and lumpy as unwashed socks.

Let's send romance out for groceries
and a tank of gas. Let's guzzle sweet tea

or warm beer straight from a dented can.
Don't promise a thing until you can look
and see space, not stars. Unstitch every last sequin

from the dress it's been hitched to. Touch
my thigh, say skin is skin, the heart a muscle. Say

your words are nothing but words; I know you
are ready to bore me right through. Now try me.
I want to try you, too.

—*Open Competition Winner*

LaWanda Walters

Her Art

I'd like to cry on Elizabeth Bishop's shoulder.
I lost my mother's engagement ring, for one thing.
Not your fault, she'd say. So much seems to want
to be lost. Even if, one day, in anger or grief
you threw it across the room or placed it somewhere
safe, the fact is, now, it's gone. Just read my poem.

Remember? My mother's watch was in that poem.
My losses are famous. Don't cry on anyone's shoulder—
even if I were available, I'm lost somewhere.
Find a nice shape and put your list of things
inside as you'd pack a valise. Be careful of your grief,
how you throw it around. People don't want

a sight like that. Write about your want
as if it were an apple or a moth. A poem,
if you're lucky, can help someone else's grief.
It might be there to lean on like a shoulder,
though that should not be your intent. My things—
why should you care at all for them or where

or why I lost them? You saw me, somewhere,
painting Florida, transcribing my want,
that perilous view, into some other thing.
It is not a raft for you to climb on. The poem
might be about someone else's shoulders,
how I miss them, perhaps, which is my grief,

not yours to worry over. Chart loss on a graph,
see how precisely rocks recall the wear
of tides and rain. Then think of those shoulders
you miss—pose them like a sculpture. The want
of arms made the Venus de Milo. A poem
is luck like that and discipline and things

you'll never have again. See those things
as tiles in a watercolor tin. Grief,
set right, can flicker and stay, and then the poem
can stand in for your lost ring. I cannot say where
to look for any of this, or if the friend you want
will disappear. Step into loss as you should—

as you like to step in water, somewhere, your shoulders
cold until you're swimming. My poem was a thing
I made, and it took some balancing, that grief and want.

—*Nominated by* The Antioch Review

Fritz Ward

Grief Is Simple Interference: Endings Overlapping

I feed the ants before I poison them.

I wrap my grief in tinsel and call the funeral director

Sugarbeets. I want to spoon her in two. One for now,

one for never. Does it matter who D-I-E-D?

After the service, there's sex and crackers and crushed

fruit. Her father snapped black and whites

of all the lilies in the room. Graveside, we shoe-gazed

and eavesdropped—Palm-sized birds and the threat

of afternoon rain. *Touch me now,* she said,

I'll freckle and tear.

—*Nominated by* Memorious

Contributors' Notes

BETH BACHMANN's poems have recently appeared in *American Poetry Review* and *The Kenyon Review,* and online at *AGNI* and *Blackbird,* among other journals. She teaches creative writing at Vanderbilt University and serves as book review editor for *The Southern Review.*

JOANN BALINGIT grew up in Polk County, Florida, and lives with her family in northern Delaware. Her poems have appeared in *Salt Hill, Smartish Pace, Pearl, Returning a Borrowed Tongue* (Coffee House Press), *DIAGRAM.2* (Del Sol Press) and elsewhere. Work is forthcoming in *On the Mason Dixon Line: Contemporary Delaware Writers* (University of Delaware Press). She's got a nerve at lafovea.org.

C. WADE BENTLEY teaches writing at Salt Lake Community College and Weber State University. His poems have appeared in *Cimarron Review, Pebble Lake Review, Green Mountains Review,* and *Jabberwock Review.* His four children and new grandson keep him from the despair that might produce better poetry.

ERIN M. BERTRAM is a fellow/instructor in the M.F.A. Writing Program at Washington University in St. Louis. Her work has appeared or is forthcoming in *Bloom, Columbia Poetry Review, CutBank, Knockout,* and *Natural Bridge.* She edits shadowbox press. Her chapbooks include *Alluvium* (dancing girl press, 2007), *Here, Hunger* (NeO Pepper Press, 2007) with Sarah Lilius, and *Body Of Water* (Thorngate Road, forthcoming), which won the 2007 Frank O'Hara Award.

CRAIG BLAIS was born and raised in Springfield, Massachusetts. He graduates from Wichita State University in December 2007. A recipient of an AWP Intro Award, his poems have appeared or are forthcoming in *Flint Hills Review, Good Foot, The Pinch, Hayden's Ferry Review,* and *The Anthology of New England Writers 2008.*

KARA CANDITO is a Ph.D. candidate in English at Florida State University, where she specializes in poetry and literary theory. Her poems and critical prose have appeared in *Poet Lore* and *The Pedestal Review.* In August 2006, she was named as a finalist in *The Florida Review* Editor's Award Contest. She lives in Tallahassee, Florida, with her two cats, Cassidy and Saturn.

NATALIE DIAZ was born and raised in the Fort Mojave Indian Village in Needles, California, and is a member of the Gila River Indian Community. After playing professional basketball in Europe and Asia, she returned to Old Dominion University to pursue her M.F.A. degree in both poetry and fiction, and graduated in May 2007. She recently won the 2007 *Nimrod*/Hardman Literary Awards Pablo Neruda Poetry Prize, the 2007 *Bellingham Review* Tobias Wolff Fiction Prize, and has work forthcoming in *The Southeast Review* (poetry), as well as *The Iowa Review* (fiction). At the moment, she resides in Surprise, Arizona, which completely suprises her.

CHRISTINA DUHIG is a recent graduate of the M.F.A. Writing Program at UNC Greensboro. Her poems have appeared in *Washington Square* and *The Greensboro Review.* She teaches at North Carolina A&T State University.

ROBIN EKISS is a former Stegner Fellow at Stanford and the recipient of a 2007 Rona Jaffe Foundation Writer's Award. Her work has appeared or is forthcoming in *The Atlantic Monthly, Poetry, TriQuarterly, Ploughshares, The Kenyon Review, New England Review, The Virginia Quarterly Review,* and elsewhere. She lives in San Francisco.

KELLY MADIGAN ERLANDSON's poems and essays have appeared in *Crazyhorse, Prairie Schooner, The Massachusetts Review,* and *32 Poems.* She has been a writer in residence at Jentel Artist Residency Program, and KHN Center for the Arts. In 2006, she was awarded the Distinguished Artist Award in Literature from the Nebraska Arts Council. She is the author of the how-to book, *Getting Sober* (McGraw-Hill, 2007).

ELYSE FENTON recently received an M.F.A. from the University of Oregon and moved to Austin, Texas. Her poetry and prose has been published or is forthcoming in *Hubbub, Salamander, Natural Bridge, The Northwest Review,* and *The Massachusetts Review.*

BRETT FOSTER's work has appeared in *AGNI, Boston Review, The Georgia Review, Hudson Review, I M A G E, The Missouri Review, Partisan Review,* and other journals. He teaches literature at Wheaton College, and is currently translating the sonnets of medieval Sienese poet Cecco Angiolieri.

LIZ GALLAGHER is Irish and lives in the Canary Islands, Spain. She has poetry, fiction, and nonfiction work published or forthcoming in *Stirring, The Pedestal Magazine, Wicked Alice, Flashquake, Kaleidowhirl, The Hiss Quarterly, Noö, Arsenic Lobster, The Mad Hatter's Review,* and others.

SCOTT GLASSMAN's most recent chapbook is *Exertions* (Cy Gist Press, 2006). His poems have appeared or are forthcoming in *Jubilat, Iowa Review, 580 Split, The Cortland Review, Jacket,* and others. He also co-curates the Emergency Reading Series in Philadelphia.

BENJAMIN GOTSCHALL grew up on a cattle ranch in the Sandhills of Holt County, Nebraska. He has an M.F.A. in creative writing from the University of Idaho. He is a visiting professor of English at Nebraska Wesleyan University in Lincoln and is the herdsman at Branched Oak Farm near Raymond, Nebraska.

ALEX GRANT's poems have appeared in numerous journals. His chapbook *Chains & Mirrors* (Harperprints) won the 2006 Randall Jarrell Poetry Prize and the 2007 Oscar Arnold Young Award (best collection by a North Carolina poet.) He received *Kakalak's* 2006 Poetry Prize and WMSU's 2004 Pavel Srut Poetry Fellowship, and has been runner-up or finalist for Discovery/*The Nation*, The Pablo Neruda, Brittingham and Pollak Prizes, and the *Arts & Letters* Poetry Prize, among others. He lives in North Carolina with his wife, Tristi.

K.A. HAYS's poems have appeared recently or are forthcoming in *The Southern Review, Missouri Review, Antioch Review, Black Warrior Review, New Orleans Review,* and other magazines. Hays is also a fiction writer and verse translator whose work in those genres has appeared in *Hudson Review, Gulf Coast, Cimarron Review,* and other magazines. She earned an M.F.A. at Brown in 2005, and currently holds the first Emerging Writer Fellowship at Bucknell University.

TODD HEARON's recent poems appear in *AGNI, Literary Imagination, Ploughshares, Poetry, Poetry London, The New Republic* and *Slate.* The winner of a 2007 PEN New England "Discovery" Award, he lives and teaches in Exeter, New Hampshire.

CHELSEA JENNINGS is an M.F.A. candidate at the University of Washington, where she also teaches creative writing. Her work has appeared in the *GW Review* and *Poet Lore.*

KRISTIN KELLY holds an M.F.A. from the Iowa Writers' Workshop. Her poems have most recently appeared or are forthcoming in *American Poetry Review, Black Warrior Review, Court Green, No Tell Motel,* and *The Tiny.* She lives in Iowa City.

ELIZABETH KNAPP holds an M.F.A. from the Bennington Writing Seminars and is currently completing a Ph.D. in creative writing at Western Michigan University. Her poems have been published in *AGNI Online, Barrow Street, Crab Orchard Review, The Massachusetts Review, Mid-American Review, Rhino,* and *Washington Square.* In 2007, she was the recipient of the Discovered Voices Award from *Iron Horse Literary Review,* where her work also appears.

Born in Singapore, JEE LEONG KOH read English at Oxford University and completed his creative writing M.F.A. at Sarah Lawrence College. His poetry chapbook, *Payday Loans,* published in April 2007, is available on his blog, http//jeeleong.blogspot.com. He now lives in New York City.

CHRISTI KRAMER was born in northern Idaho and is a graduate of George Mason University's Graduate Creative Writing Program. The poem "Biography of *awe,*" is from her manuscript, *Reading The Throne,* an ethnography-in-poetry of Iraqi Kurds exiled and living as refugees in Harrisonburg, Virginia.

ELIZABETH LANGEMAK lives in Columbia, Missouri. Her work has appeared or is forthcoming in journals such as *Gulf Coast, The Crab Orchard Review, Ninth Letter,* and *The Cincinnati Review.*

NATALIE LYALIN lives in Philadelphia where she coedits *Glitterpony* magazine. Her work has appeared in *Skein, Unpleasant Events Schedule, Octopus,* and *Coconut.* Natalie teaches composition at Temple University.

ED MADDEN teaches at the University of South Carolina and serves as writer in residence at Riverbanks Botanical Gardens. His first book, *Signals,* won the 2007 South Carolina Book Prize and will be published by USC Press in 2008. "Sacrifice" was also selected for *The Book of Irish American Poetry from the Eighteenth Century to the Present* (Notre Dame, 2007).

DORA MALECH is currently a visiting lecturer and primary convenor for the M.A. Writing Program at Victoria University's Institute of Modern Letters in Wellington, New Zealand. She received her B.A. from Yale and her M.F.A. from the Iowa Writers' Workshop. Her poems have appeared or are forthcoming in numerous publications, including *American Letters & Commentary, Denver Quarterly, Gulf Coast, LIT,* and *Poetry.*

MICHELLE MCEWEN lives, dreams, and writes in Central Connecticut. A very northern girl with very southern parents, she has plenty material for poetry. She holds a B.A. in English Writing from the University of Pittsburgh and has had several poems published in university literary magazines; her poem "Orange Lover" appeared online in the spring 2007 issue of BigCityLit.com.

TYLER MILLS is finishing an M.F.A. in poetry at the University of Maryland where she is assistant director of the Writing Center. She was awarded the *Gulf Coast* poetry prize for 2006 and her work has also recently appeared in *Indiana Review.* She enjoys playing the violin.

TOMAS Q. MORIN was educated at Texas State University and Johns Hopkins University. His poems have appeared or are forthcoming in *Ploughshares, New Orleans Review, Boulevard,* and *Slate.*

LAURA NEWBERN's full-length collection, *Love and the Eye,* has been a finalist for the Walt Whitman Award and the *Verse* Prize, among others. She teaches at Georgia College & State University and is the poetry editor of *Arts & Letters.*

MATTHEW NIENOW's work has appeared or is forthcoming in several magazines, including *American Literary Review, Poet Lore,* and *Atlanta Review,* among others. His chapbook, *Two Sides Of The Same Thing,* won the 2007 Copperdome Prize and is available from Southeast Missouri State University Press.

JULIE SOPHIA PAEGLE's poems have appeared in *Cream City Review, Ploughshares, Prairie Schooner, The Iowa Review, The Southern Review, Colorado Review, Third Coast, New Orleans Review, Barrow Street,* and *Alpinist,* among others. She is an assistant professor of poetry at California State University, San Bernardino and lives with her husband and sons in Angelus Oaks, California.

CECILY PARKS's first collection, *Field Folly Snow,* will be published by the University of Georgia Press *VQR* Poetry Series in 2008. Her chapbook *Cold Work* was published in 2005 by the Poetry Society of America. She is currently a Ph.D. candidate in English at the CUNY Graduate Center in New York. The last line of "The Fern Seed" comes from Thoreau.

SARAH PERRIER is the author of a chapbook, *Just One of Those Things.* Other publication credits include *Hotel Amerika, The Journal, Pleiades,* and *Mid-American Review.* She lives in Pennsylvania and teaches creative writing and literature at the University of Pittsburgh at Bradford. Her manuscript *Nothing Fatal* has been a finalist for the

Tupelo Press First Book of Poetry Contest and the National Poetry Series, as well as a semifinalist for BOA Editions' first-book prize.

CATHERINE PIERCE is the author of *Famous Last Words,* winner of the 2007 Saturnalia Books Poetry Prize (forthcoming January 2008), as well as a chapbook, *Animals of Habit* (Kent State 2004). She is an assistant professor of creative writing at Mississippi State University.

CHRISTINE RHEIN is the seventeenth winner of the Walt McDonald First-Book Competition in Poetry. Her collection, *Wild Flight,* will be published by Texas Tech University Press in Spring 2008. A former mechanical engineer, she lives in Brighton, Michigan, with her husband and their two sons. Her poems have appeared in many journals, including *The Gettysburg Review, The Southern Review,* and *Michigan Quarterly Review,* where her poem "One of those questions" won the 2006 Laurence Goldstein Poetry Prize.

MARGARET RONDA's poems have appeared in journals such as *AGNI, Pool, Xantippe, Prairie Schooner, Fourteen Hills,* and *The Seattle Review.* She is a doctoral candidate in English at the University of California-Berkeley and currently resides in Oregon.

DONIKA ROSS is James A. Michener Fellow in poetry at the Michener Center for Writers. Other poems appear or are forthcoming in *Temba Tupu! (Walking Naked) The Africana Woman's Poetic Self Portrait,* and *Ellipsis.*

JAIME ROSS writes—and paints—on a mesa west of Taos, New Mexico. His work has appeared in *5AM, BPJ, Nimrod, Margie, Runes, The Paris Review, Five Fingers, Western Humanities, Sulphur River, Comstock, Marlboro, The Texas Review,* and *Northwest Review.* Two collections, *Postcards From Mexico,* and the more recent *Bringing In The Name* are currently coursing toward a publisher.

ROBERT SAWYER was a winner of the 2003 Discovery/*The Nation* Contest. When not writing poetry, he masquerades as a creative strategist. In that guise he has conceived communications for some of the world's largest companies, as well as some you'd need a séance to find. Sawyer lives in New York City with his wife, the editor Chalotte Barnard.

ROBIN BETH SCHAER is the recipient of fellowships from the Saltonstall Foundation and the Virginia Center for the Creative Arts, and was a finalist for the 2006 Kinereth Gensler Award from Alice James Books. Her work has appeared in *Denver Quarterly, Rattapallax, From the Fishouse, Drunken Boat, Barrow Street,* and *Greensboro Review,* among others. She works at the Academy of American Poets and lives in New York City.

MORGAN LUCAS SCHULDT is the author of *Verge* (Parlor Press: Free Verse Editions, forthcoming fall, 2007) and *Otherhow,* a chapbook now out from Kitchen Press. His work has appeared most recently in *Fence, Verse,* and *Coconut.* He lives in Arizona where he edits *CUE: A Journal of Prose Poetry.*

BRANDON SOM lives and writes in Pittsburgh, Pennsylvania. His work has appeared in such journals as *Barrow Street, Octopus Magazine,* and *McSweeney's.*

REBECCA WADLINGER is a James A. Michener Fellow in poetry and playwriting at the University of Texas at Austin. A 2005 June Fellow in the Bucknell Seminar for Younger Poets, her writing has appeared in *Pebble Lake Review, Verse Daily,* and *The Cimarron Review.*

LAWANDA WALTERS teaches at the University of Cincinnati. Her poems have appeared in *Antioch Review, Ploughshares, Laurel Review, Southern Poetry Review,* and *Cincinnati Review.* She received her M.F.A. from Indiana University and won the Academy of American Poets Prize while she was there.

FRITZ WARD's poems have appeared in more than forty-five journals, including *American Arts and Commentary, AGNI, Swink, Salt Hill, Diagram, No Tell Motel, Portland Review,* and *The Journal.* He holds an M.F.A. in creative writing from the

University of North Carolina Greensboro. He currently lives in Santa Rosa, California.

DAVID WELCH holds a Teaching Writing Fellowship at the University of Alabama where he currently serves as poetry editor of *Black Warrior Review*. His poems have appeared most recently in *Pleiades, Pebble Lake Review,* and *New Orleans Review*.

JORDAN WINDHOLZ lives with his wife in Boulder, Colorado. He has recent poems published or forthcoming in *Nimrod, Denver Quarterly, Pebble Lake Review,* and *Diner*. He has also been nominated for a Pushcart Prize.

GRETA WROLSTAD passed away on August 9, 2005 from injuries suffered in a car accident. A thinker, adventurer, traveler and observer, she pursued an M.F.A. degree in creative writing at the University of Montana, where she also served as poetry coeditor of *CutBank*. Greta attended the 2005 Summer Literary Seminars in St. Petersburg, Russia, on a scholarship awarded by Fence Books. Her poems have been published in *The Canary, Black Warrior Review,* and *CutBank*.

Acknowledgments

Beth Bachmann's "Nesting" previously published in *Black Warrior Review*.

C. Wade Bentley's "Fortune" previously published in *Cimarron Review*.

Erin M. Bertram's "[Mesmerist]" previously published in *Natural Bridge*.

Craig Blais's "Sister at the Airport" previously published in *Eclipse*.

Natalie Diaz's "Why I Don't Mention Flowers When Conversations with My Brother Reach Uncomfortable Silences" previously published in *Southeast Review*.

Christina Duhig's "What Places, Things" previously published in *Washington Square*.

Robin Ekiss's "Vanitas Mundi" previously published in *The Virginia Quarterly Review*.

Kelly Madigan Erlandson's "Reliquary" previously published in *The Eleventh Muse*.

Brett Foster's "The First Request of Lazarus" previously published in *I M A G E* and *American Religious Poems*.

Liz Gallagher's "A Poem That Thinks It Has Joined a Circus" previously published on Interboard Poetry Community, http://www.webdelsol.com/IBPC

Scott Glassman's "Drinks over the Medusa Fossae" previously published in *Web del Sol*.

Alex Grant's "The Steps of Montmartre" previously published in *Poemeleon: A Journal of Poetry*.

K.A. Hays's "Serotinous" previously published in *Black Warrior Review*.

Todd Hearon's "In the Garden" previously published in *Harvard Review*.

Chelsea Jennings's "Landing" previously published in *GW Review*.

Jee Leong Koh's "Brother" previously published in *The Ledge Magazine*

Christi Kramer's "Biography of *awe*" previously published in *PRACTICE: NEW WRITING + ART*.

Ed Madden's "Sacrifice" previously published in *The Book of Irish American Poetry from the Eighteenth Century to the Present*.

Tyler Mills's "Violin Shop" previously published in *Indiana Review*.

Matthew Nienow's "Six Ways of Looking at the Moon" previously published in *Eclipse*.

Julie Sophia Paegle's "Clock & Echo" previously published in *The Cream City Review*.

Cecily Parks's "The Fern Seed" previously published in *River Styx*.

Catherine Pierce's "Epithalamium" previously published in *Third Coast*.

Christine Rhein's "One of those questions" previously published in *Michigan Quarterly Review*.

Margaret Ronda's "Walking Late" previously published in *The Eleventh Muse*.

Donika Ross's "Ceremony" previously published in *Ellipsis*.

Jamie Ross's "Peterbilt" previously published in *Northwest Review*.

Robin Beth Schaer's "The Liger" previously published in *The Greensboro Review*.

Morgan Lucas Schuldt's "Triptych for Francis Bacon" previously published in *Sentence*.

LaWanda Walters's "Her Art" previously published in *The Antioch Review*.

Fritz Ward's "Grief Is Simple Interference: Endings Overlapping" previously published in *Memorius*.

David Welch's "Tribute" previously published in *New Orleans Review*.

Greta Wrolstad's "Notes on Sea and Shore" previously published in *Black Warrior Review*.

Participating Writing Programs

American University
M.F.A. Program in Creative Writing
Department of Literature
4400 Massachusetts Avenue N.W.
Washington, DC 20036

The Bread Loaf Writers' Conference
Middlebury College
Kirk Alumni Center
Middlebury, VT 05753
www.middlebury.edu

Brooklyn College
M.F.A. Program in Creative Writing
Department of English
2900 Bedford Avenue
Brooklyn, NY 11210

Brown University
Program in Literary Arts
Box 1923
Providence, RI 02912
www.brown.edu/Departments/Literary_Arts

Columbia University Writing Division
School of the Arts
Dodge Hall
2960 Broadway, Room 400
New York, NY 10027-6902

Eastern Washington University
Creative Writing Program
MS #1
705 West First Avenue
Spokane, WA 99201-3909

Emerson College
M.F.A. in Creative Writing
120 Boylston Street
Boston, MA 02116-1596

Fine Arts Work Center in Provincetown
Writing Fellowship
24 Pearl Street
Provincetown, MA 02657
www.fawc.org

Florida International University
M.F.A. Program in Creative Writing
Department of English, Biscayne Bay Camp
3000 N.E. 151st Street
North Miami, FL 33181

Florida State University
Department of English
Williams Building
Tallahassee, FL 32306-1580
english.fsu.edu/crw/index.html

George Mason University
Creative Writing Program
4400 University Drive
MS 3E4
Fairfax, VA 22030
creativewriting.gmu.edu

Goddard College
M.F.A. in Creative Writing
123 Pitkin Road
Plainfield, VT 05667
www.goddard.edu

Hollins University
Creative Writing Program
P.O. Box 9677
Roanoke, VA 24020

Kalamazoo College
Writing Program
English Department
1200 Academy Street
Kalamazoo, MI 49006
www.kzoo.edu/programs

Kundiman Asian American Poetry Retreat
245 Eight Avenue, #151
New York, NY 10011

The Loft Literary Center
Mentor Series Program
Suite 200, Open Book
1011 Washington Avenue
South Minneapolis, MN 55414-1246
www.loft.org

Louisiana State University
English Department
260 Allen
Baton Rouge, LA 70803
english.lsu.edu/dept/programs/
    creative_writing

McNeese State University
Program in Creative Writing
P.O. Box 92655
Lake Charles, LA 70609
www.mfa.mcneese.edu

Mills College
Master of Fine Arts
Mills Hall Rm 303
5000 MacArthur Blvd.
Oakland, CA 94613

Minnesota State University, Mankato
Creative Writing Program
230 Armstrong Hall
Mankato, MN 56001
www.english.mnsu.edu

New Mexico State University
Department of English
Box 30001
Department 3E
Las Cruces, NM 88003-8001
www.nmsu.edu

The New School
Graduate Writing Program
66 West 12th Street, Room 505
New York, NY 10001

Oberlin College
Creative Writing Program
Rice Hall 11
Oberlin College
Oberlin, OH 44074
www.oberlin.edu/crwrite

Ohio State University
Creative Writing Program
Department of English, 421 Denney Hall
164 West 17th Avenue
Columbus, OH 43210-1370

Pacific University
Master of Fine Arts in Creative Writing
2403 College Way
Forest Grove, OR 97116
www.pacificu.edu/as/mfa

Saint Mary's College of California
M.F.A. Program in Creative Writing
P.O. Box 4686
Moraga, CA 94575-4686
www.stmarys-ca.edu/academics

San Diego State University
M.F.A. Program
Department of English and
    Comparative Literature
5500 Campanile Drive
San Diego, CA 92182-8140

San Francisco State University
Creative Writing Department
College of Humanities
1600 Holloway Avenue
San Francisco, CA 94132-4162

Sarah Lawrence College
Office of Graduate Studies
1 Mead Way
Bronxville, NY 10708-5999

Sewanee Writers' Conference
735 University Avenue
Sewanee, TN 37383-1000
www.sewaneewriters.org

Texas A&M University
Creative Writing Program
Deptartment of English
Blocker 227 – TAMU 4227
College Station, TX 77843-4227

Texas State University
M.F.A. Program in Creative Writing
Department of English
601 University Drive, Flowers Hall
San Marcos, TX 78666
www.txstate.edu

Texas Tech University
Creative Writing Program
English Department
TTU
Lubbock, TX 79409-3091
www.english.ttu.edu/cw

University of Alabama
Program in Creative Writing
Department of English
P.O. Box 870244
Tuscaloosa, AL 35487-0244
www.bama.ua.edu/~writing

University of Alaska
Fairbanks Program in Creative Writing
Department of English
P.O. Box 755720
Fairbanks, AK 99775-5720
www.uaf.edu/english

University of Arizona
Creative Writing Program
Department of English
Modern Languages Building #67
Tucson, AZ 85721-0067

University of Arkansas
Program in Creative Writing
Department of English
333 Kimpel Hall
Fayetteville, AR 72701
www.uark.edu/depts/english/PCWT.html

University of California, Davis
Graduate Creative Writing Program
Department of English
Davis, CA 95616

University of Colorado at Boulder
Creative Writing Program
Department of English
Campus Box 226
Boulder, CO 80309-0226

University of Denver
Creative Writing Program
Department of English
2140 South Race Street
Denver, CO 80208
www.du.edu/english/gradcwr.html

University of Florida
Creative Writing Program
Department of English
P.O. Box 11730
Gainesville, FL 32611-7310
www.english.ufl.edu/crw/

University of Georgia
Creative Writing Program
English Department
Park Hall 111
Athens, GA 30602-6205

University of Hawaii
Creative Writing Program
English Department
1733 Donaghho Road
Honolulu, HI 96822
www.english.hawaii.edu/cw

University of Idaho
Creative Writing Program
Department of English
Moscow, ID 83843-1102
www.class.uidaho.edu/english/CW/
    mfaprogram.html

University of Illinois at Chicago
Program for Writers
Department of English MC/162
601 South Morgan Street
Chicago, IL 60607-7120
www.uic.edu/english

University of Maryland
Creative Writing Program
Department of English
3119F Susquehanna Hall
College Park, MD 20742
www.english.umd.edu/programs/
    CreateWriting/index.html

University of Massachusetts
M.F.A. Program for Poets and Writers
Bartlett Hall
130 Hicks Way
Amherst, MA 01003-9269

University of Minnesota
M.F.A. Program in Creative Writing
Department of English
207 Church Street
SE Minneapolis, MN 55455
english.cla.umn.edu/creativewriting/
    program.html

University of Missouri-Columbia
Program in Creative Writing
Department of English
107 Tate Hall
Columbia, MO 65211
www.missouri.edu/~cwp

University of Missouri-St. Louis
M.F.A. in Creative Writing Program
Department of English
8001 Natural Bridge Road
St. Louis, MO 63121
www.umsl.edu/~mfa

University of North Carolina, Greensboro
M.F.A. Writing Program
Dept. of English, 134 McIver Building
P.O. Box 26170
Greensboro, NC 27402-6170
www.uncg.edu/eng/mfa

University of North Texas
Department of English
P.O. Box 311307
Denton, TX 76203-1307
www.engl.unt.edu/grad/grad_creative.htm

University of Notre Dame
Creative Writing Program
356 O'Shaughnessy Hall
Notre Dame, IN 46556-0368
www.nd.edu/~alcwp

University of Oregon
Program in Creative Writing
5243 University of Oregon
Eugene, OR 97403-5243
darkwing.uoregon.edu/~crwrweb

University of San Francisco
Master of Arts in Writing Program
Program Office, Lone Mountain 340
2130 Fulton Street
San Francisco, CA 94117-1080

University of Texas
Michener Center for Writers
J. Frank Dobie House
702 East Dean Keeton Street
Austin, TX 78705
www.utexas.edu/academic/mcw

University of Utah
Creative Writing Program
255 South Central Campus Drive
Room 3500
Salt Lake City, UT 84112

University of Virginia
Creative Writing Program
Department of English
P.O. Box 400121
Charlottesville, VA 22904-4121
www.engl.virginia.edu/cwp

University of Washington
Creative Writing Program
Box 354330
Seattle, WA 98195-4330

University of Wisconsin-Madison
Wisconsin Institute for Creative Writing
Department of English
Helen C. White Hall
Madison, WI 53706
creativewriting.wisc.edu

University of Wisconsin-Madison
M.F.A. in Creative Writing
Department of English
600 N. Park St.
Madison, WI 53706

University of Wisconsin-Milwaukee
Creative Writing Program
Department of English Box 413
Milwaukee, WI 53201

University of Wyoming
Creative Writing Program
Department of English
P.O. Box 3353
Laramie, WY 82071-2000
www.uwyo.edu/creativewriting

Vermont College
Master of Fine Arts in Writing
36 College Street
Montpelier, VT 05602
www.tui.edu

Virginia Commonwealth University
M.F.A. in Creative Writing Program
Department of English
P.O. Box 842005
Richmond, VA 23284-2005

Wesleyan Writers Conference
Weslyan University
294 High Street, Room 204
Middletown, CT 06459

West Virginia University
Creative Writing Program
Department of English
P.O. Box 6269
Morgantown, WV 26506-6269
www.as.wvu.edu/english

Western Michigan University
Graduate Program in Creative Writing
Department of English
Kalamazoo, MI 49008-5092

Wichita State University
M.F.A. in Creative Writing
1845 North Fairmount
Wichita, KS 67260-0014
webs.wichita.edu/cwfwww

Canada

The Humber School for Writers
Correspondence Program in Creative Writing
205 Humber College Boulevard
Humber College
Toronto, ON M9W 5L7
www.humber.ca/creativeandperformingarts

University of British Columbia
Creative Writing Program
Buchanan E462-1866 Main Mall
Vancouver, BC V6T 1Z1
www.creativewriting.ubc.ca

University of Calgary
Creative Writing Research Group (CWRG)
English Department
Creative Writing Program
Calgary, AB T2N 1N4
www.english.ucalgary.ca/creative

University of Victoria
Bachelor of Fine Arts
Department of Writing
P.O. Box 1700, STN CSC
Victoria, BC V8W 2Y2

Participating Magazines

32 Poems Magazine
P.O. Box 5824
Hyattsville, MD 20782
www.32poems.com

AGNI
Boston University
236 Bay State Road
Boston, MA 02215
www.bu.edu/agni

Alaska Quarterly Review
University of Alaska, Anchorage
3211 Providence Drive
Anchorage, AK 99508

Alligator Juniper
Prescott College
220 Grove Avenue
Prescott, AZ 86301
www.prescott.edu/highlights/alligator_juniper

The Antioch Review
Antioch University
P.O. Box 148
Yellow Springs, OH 45387
www.review.antioch.edu

Bellevue Literary Review
NYU School of Medicine
Department of Medicine
550 First Avenue, OBV-A612
New York, NY 10016
www.BLReview.org

Beloit Poetry Journal
The Beloit Poetry Journal Foundation, Inc.
P.O. Box 151
Farmington, ME 04938
www.bpj.org

The Bitter Oleander
4983 Tall Oaks Drive
Fayetteville, NY 13066-9776
www.bitteroleander.com

Black Warrior Review
University of Alabama
Box 862936
Tuscaloosa, AL 35486
www.webdelsol.com/bwr

Blackbird
Virginia Commonwealth University
Department of English
P.O. Box 843082
Richmond, VA 23284-3082
www.blackbird.vcu.edu

Blue Mesa Review
University of New Mexico
MSC03-2170, Humanities 274
Creative Writing Program
Albuquerque, NM 87131
www.unm.edu/~bluemesa

Boxcar Poetry Review
146 McAllister St., #506
San Francisco, CA 94102
www.boxcarpoetry.com

*Calyx, A Journal of Art and Literature
    by Women*
P.O. Box B
Corvallis, OR 97339
www.calyxpress.org

Cave Wall
P.O. Box 29546
Greensboro, NC 27429-9546
www.cavewallpress.com

The Cream City Review
University of Milwaukee-Wisconsin
Department of English
P.O. Box 413
Milwaukee, WI 53201
www.uwm.edu/Dept/English/ccr

The Eleventh Muse
Poetry West
P.O. Box 2413
Colorado Springs, CO 80901
www.poetrywest.org/muse.htm

FIELD
Oberlin College Press
50 North Professor Street
Oberlin, OH 44074
www.oberlin.edu/ocpress

The Georgia Review
University of Georgia
Gilbert Hall 012
Athens, GA 30602-9009
www.uga.edu/garev

The Gettysburg Review
Gettysburg College
300 N. Washington Street
Gettysburg, PA 17325-1491
www.gettysburgreview.com

The Greensboro Review
University of North Carolina, Greensboro
MFA Writing Program
3302 Hall for Humanities and Research
Administration
Greensboro, NC 27402-6170
www.uncg.edu/eng/mfa

Gulf Coast
University of Houston
Department of English
Houston, TX 77204-3013
www.gulfcoastmag.org

Harvard Review
Harvard University
Lamont Library
Cambridge, MA 02138
hcl.harvard.edu/harvardreview

The Hudson Review
684 Park Avenue
New York, NY 10021
www.hudsonreview.com

Hunger Mountain
Vermont College
36 College Street
Montpelier, VT 05602
www.hungermtn.org

I M A G E
3307 Third Avenue West
Seattle, WA 98119
www.imagejournal.org

Indiana Review
Ballantine Hall 465
1020 E. Kirkwood Ave.
Bloomington, IN 47405-7103
www.indiana.edu/~inreview

The Kenyon Review
Kenyon College
Walton House
Gambier, OH 43022-9623
www.kenyonreview.org

The Ledge Magazine
40 Maple Avenue
Bellport, NY 11713
www.theledgemagazine.com

Memorious
14 Laurel St.
Cambridge, MA 02139
www.memorious.org
Michigan Quarterly Review

Michigan Quarterly Review
University of Michigan
3574 Rackham Building
915 East Washington St.
Ann Arbor, MI 48019-1070
www.umich.edu/~mqr

Mid-American Review
Bowling Green State University
Department of English
Box W
Bowling Green, OH 43403
www.bgsu.edu/midamericanreview

Mississippi Review
The University of Southern Mississippi
Box 5144
Hattiesburg, MS 39406-0001
www.mississippireview.com

The Missouri Review
University of Missouri
1507 Hillcrest Hall
Columbia, MO 65211

The National Poetry Review
P.O. Box 2080
Aptos, CA 95001-2080
www.nationalpoetryreview.com

New Letters
University of Missouri-Kansas City
5101 Rockhill Road
Kansas City, MO 64110
www.newletters.org

Nimrod
The University of Tulsa
600 South College
Tulsa, OK 74104-3189
www.utulsa.edu/nimrod

Ninth Letter
234 English, University of Illinois
608 S. Wright St.
Urbana, IL 61801
www.ninthletter.com

No Tell Motel
c/o Reb Livingston
11436 Fairway Drive
Reston, VA 20190
www.notellmotel.org

Northwest Review
University of Oregon
369 PLC New Line
Eugene, OR 97403
nwr.uoregon.edu

Pebble Lake Review
15318 Pebble Lake Dr.
Houston, TX 77095
www.pebblelakereview.com

Phoebe
George Mason University
4400 University Drive
Fairfax, VA 22030-4444

Pleiades
Central Missouri State University
Department of English and Philosophy
Martin 336
Warrensburg, MO 64093
www.cmsu.edu/englphil/pleiades

Ploughshares
Emerson College
120 Boylston St.
Boston, MA 02116
www.pshares.org

Poemeleon: A Journal of Poetry
3509 Bryce Way
Riverside, CA 92506
www.poemeleon.org

PRACTICE: NEW WRITING + ART
Practice Press, Inc.
56 Walnut Ave
Mill Valley, CA 94941
http://www.practicejournal.com

River Styx
Big River Association
3547 Olive Street Suite 107
Saint Louis, MO 63103
www.riverstyx.org

Sentence
Firewheel Editions
Box 7
181 White St.
Danbury, CT 06810
www.firewheel-editions.org

Shenandoah
Washington and Lee University
Mattingly House
2 Lee Avenue
Lexington, VA 24450-0303
shenandoah.wlu.edu

Smartish Pace
Smartish Pace, Inc.
P.O. Box 22161
Baltimore, MD 21203
www.smartishpace.com

The Southeast Review
Florida State University
English Department
Tallahassee, FL 32306
www.southeastreview.org

The Southern Review
Louisiana State University
Old President's House
Baton Rouge, LA 70803
www.lsu.edu/thesouthernreview

The Southwest Review
Southern Methodist University
307 Fondren Library West
P.O. Box 750374
Dallas, TX 75275-0374
www.southwestreview.org

Stirring : A Literary Collection
Sundress Publications
604 N. 31st Ave
Apt. C6
Hattiesburg, MS 39401
www.sundress.net/stirring

Streetlight Magazine
Charlottesville Writing Center
P.O. Box 259
Charlottesville, VA 22902

Three Candles Journal
P.O. Box 1817
Burnsville, MN 55337
www.threecandles.org

upstreet
Ledgetop Publishing
P.O. Box 105
205 Summit Road
Richmond, MA 01254-0105
www.upstreet-mag.org

Verse
University of Georgia
Department of English
Athens, GA 30602
www.versemag.blogspot.com

The Virginia Quarterly Review
University of Virginia
One West Range
P.O. Box 400223
Charlottesville, VA 22904
www.vqronline.org

Web del Sol
2020 Pennsylvania Ave., NW
Suite 443
Washington, DC 20006

ZYZZYVA
P.O. Box 590069
San Francisco, CA 94159-0069
www.zyzzyva.org

Canada

Event
Douglas College
Box 2503
New Wesminster, BC V3L 5B2
event.douglas.bc.ca